The Fruit Trees Book: Growing Orange & Citrus Trees – Blood Oranges, Navel, Valencia, Clementine, Cara And More

DIY Planting, Irrigation, Fertilizing, Pest Prevention, Leaf Sampling & Soil Analysis

VAS BLAGODARSKIY

ISBN-13: 978-1949727067
ISBN-10: 1949727068

CONTENTS

Introduction

When you want to enjoy the taste of a fresh citrus fruit, whether it is squeezing your own orange juice, or adding a dash of lemon to your favorite dish, you probably run off to the produce aisle and pick something that looks like the best of the bunch.

You don't stop to wonder if the fruit was sprayed with preservatives and pest sprays, or if it's not as fresh as the label would have you believe. You probably don't know that some citrus fruits are dyed to give them that deep, beautiful coloration. Not to mention, the number of hands that touch it before it gets to your table. "If it looks good, it must be good."

What if I told you that you can grow citrus trees in your own backyard or even start a small balcony orchard, and that it's not as complicated as you would think? All you need is soil, plants, commitment, and a guide book to show you the way.

Well, this is that guide book! With a little know how, you can grow your citrus trees just about anywhere, even indoors. This guide will help you through the critical stages in your tree's development and have you harvesting your own fruits in the blink of an eye. If you get good value from this book, please remember to leave it a great review on Amazon or wherever you bought it.

Before we get into it: Quick special thanks to my editor Becky and the Amazon support team for helping me get these books up and running! I would not be able to do this endeavor without your help.

Once you have mastered growing one type of citrus fruit, you'll see that they all are quite similar to grow. Later in this book, you will learn the technical side of growing your own citrus trees at home, including the layout of the orchard, climate requirements, irrigation techniques, leaf sampling, planting tips, and more to help your citrus tree survive and thrive for many years of fresh, homegrown citrus fruits.

Ready to get started? Let's begin the journey with growing your own orange and blood orange trees.

Orange Trees

When people think about citrus fruits, the first one to come to mind will most likely be oranges. And why not? The orange is a juicy, tasty and nutritious snack right off the tree, and can be made into a wonderful refreshing beverage for breakfast, or turned into a fruit salad for any time of day. Mix them into smoothies, or even fruit pies; the orange is incredibly versatile and best of all, it can be grown in your own back yard.

While you can plant an orange tree from seed, these trees will be at a higher risk for diseases and have a shorter life span. If they do survive the most critical part of their growth period, they will be much slower to mature and bear fruit, a process that can take up to fifteen years. Take heart, citrus grower; professional orange growers have a secret weapon called grafting. Grafting is the process of taking a desired variety of plant or fruit called a scion, in this case an orange tree, and attaching it to a seedling that is already established, called a rootstock. This process is known as budding, and it gives your orange tree a jump start on growth. A grafted tree will grow much faster than a seed grown tree, and you can get them at local nurseries. When choosing your grafted tree, make sure it isn't overly large or aged; these trees will most likely be pot-bound and not do well after planting.

After the orange tree has been planted, there are three key requirements to keep it growing healthy and strong.

Watering

Your orange tree will require watering on a regular basis. How much watering is needed will vary by your individual rainfall and climate. Each spring, a regular watering schedule is needed to keep the tree's leaves from drooping and wilting while every fall, watering will need to be restricted.

Too much water will lower the solidness of your fruit by increase its liquid content. It's not rocket science, just basic physics. More water in, more juice out.

Fertilizing

Fertilizing your orange tree will affect the quality of the fruit rind, so you may need higher or lower levels of some nutrients depending on what your orange's intended usage. Potassium fertilizer, for instance, will result in a peel with lower levels of oils, while fertilizer containing extra nitrogen will increase the levels of oil in the skin.

To increase the yields of the orange trees, it is recommended that between one to two pounds of nitrogen should be added to the tree annually. A complete fertilizer should be used, complete with a full variety of micro-nutrients, phosphorous, and potassium. You can increase fertilization by applying a compound directly to the tree's leaves a few times per year. If an older fruit tree is beginning to slow down its yield, a soil test is needed to define if any additional fertilization requirements are needed.

Pruning your Orange Tree

Your orange tree will need to be pruned to increase light penetration through the branches, allowing the fruit to benefit from light and aeration. As with just about any other tree, all diseased or dead branches should be removed on a regular basis. However, citrus trees do not generally require shaping. In addition, all branches below two feet from the ground should be removed to encourage the tree's upward and outward growth. Skirt pruning will offer protection from diseases that are passed to the tree from the soil and make laying mulch or pulling weeds much easier.

Pruning your citrus trees makes harvesting your yield much easier, and a shorter tree will reduce the risk of injury that could occur from falling from a ladder while picking the fruit. Unlike other fruit trees, citrus trees seldom need to have their fruits thinned out unless the weight of the fruit is damaging the branches.

Citrus trees can be grown as an espalier, in a pot, or shaped as a hedge if they are pruned properly, making it possible to grow them in more limited spaces. Potted citrus plants will seldom need to be pruned because they will only grow to the space allowed by their container. They may still need pruning to remove any dying or damaged branches, to allow light and aeration to reach the fruit, and to remove any sprouts growing below the graft.

Harvesting your Oranges

Nothing is more rewarding than enjoying the "fruits of your labors," but how do you know when will your oranges are ready for harvesting?

Color is not always the best way to judge the ripeness of your fruit, as you have learned from picking fruit from the produce aisle. In fact, grocers and fruit stands can dye the fruit to give it that deep orange color we associate with freshness.

Orange yields will largely depend on the variety of tree that you have planted. The harvest can occur from March to January, so it's important to understand yield times of the individual variety of your tree. As a broad rule, most orange trees yield fruit from September through early spring time. Here are a few popular varieties and their yield times:

Clementine oranges: October through December or January

Valencia oranges: March through October

Satsuma oranges: October through December or January

Pineapple sweet oranges: November through February

Cara oranges: December through May

Navel oranges: November through June

Blood Oranges

A blood orange tree, genus *Citrus sinensis*, is an Asian citrus variety that is smaller in size than a navel orange and shares its bright orange rind with its cousins. Once a blood orange is sliced, however, the difference is clear: its fruit is a brilliant red hue, blood-like in color. The coloration is in the pulp and juices as well as the fruit. It is a popular citrus fruit, prized for its rind, fruit, juice and pulp which are much sweeter than a common orange. The blood orange is easy to peel and contains far fewer seeds than its citrus cousins. It is used in deserts and is a great complement to seafood dishes.

Growing Blood Oranges

While the blood oranges are best suited to be grown in warmer, temperate climates (US climate zones 9-10) with temperatures between 55-85 degrees Fahrenheit, it is also a great little tree for containers. Blood orange trees in containers can be moved inside to a location with lots of light and an average temperature of around 65 degrees Fahrenheit. When growing the tree inside, keep the container a full two feet away from the window because the glass can magnify the heat on your tree's leaves.

If you are planting your blood orange tree outdoors, aim for a March planting, after all dangers of frost are over for the season. The ideal spot for a blood orange tree will get full sun throughout the day. It prefers a soil with excellent water drainage, so adding organic compost or peat moss equally proportionate to your soil is a good idea. When planting, make sure the roots are the only part of the tree covered by the soil and keep all of its trunk above the soil level.

Caring for your Blood Orange Tree

When bringing your blood orange tree inside for the winter, remember to keep it in a sunny location in your home and add humidity to the tree to keep it lush and growing. If your tree is wintering outside, keep the trunk wrapped up with plastic or blankets and give it a good layer of mulch to protect it against frost and temperature extremes.

When the tree is established, keep the soil moist and not overly wet. During seasons of rain, you will be able to skip watering the tree altogether. Your blood orange tree will require feeding several times a year. Choose an organic fertilizer to place in the soil around the tree, or consider using a liquid fertilizer every other watering, following the directions on the label. Make sure your fertilizer has high levels of zinc, iron and manganese for the healthiest fruits. If you find your leaves yellowing, you may need more water or more fertilization.

Blood orange trees should only be pruned to their area of planting or their container size. Prune heavy growth at the level of the tips to keep the tree to a manageable height. Potted blood orange trees should be removed from their pots to access their roots every few years; cut about one third of the root system, add fertilized and balanced soil, and replant it in its container. Gloves are recommended when you are working around your blood orange tree because some varieties have sharp spines.

Your blood orange tree will produce many sweet-smelling flowers in the spring and will continue to bloom intermittently the rest of the year. The blooming season is a true beauty to behold.

Harvesting Your Oranges

It's not always easy to know when it's time to harvest your oranges. While color isn't always a good indication of ripeness, picking green fruit is never a good choice. Unlike other fruits, citrus fruits won't continue to ripen on your counter after being picked. Generally speaking, the deeper orange or yellow the orange's skin appears, the riper it is and the sweeter the fruit will taste. The best way to see if your oranges are ready to be picked is to pick a couple and see how they taste. The process of harvesting is easy; just grab the orange and twist it until it pulls free from the stem. Fruit that is higher in the tree can be shaken down by standing on a ladder and moving the branches briskly. If the rinds of your oranges are thin or tear easily, use a pair of clippers and cut the stems instead of twisting the fruit or shaking them free.

Many varieties of oranges should be picked on an as-needed basis, with the rest remaining in the tree. This is a natural method to store them, and they will grow even sweeter if they are still on the tree. Keep an eye on the fruit and discard any that is diseased and avoid any oranges that smell off. A ripe fruit will be firm and smell of fresh, sweet oranges. A sickly orange will be blemished or show signs of fungus or mold. Any fruit that drops naturally from the tree is completely edible if it is free of mold, fungus, blemishes or torn skins.

If you find that your oranges are too watery and have a sour or bitter taste, there are a few ways you can ensure your future yields are healthier.

- **Location of your trees:** Because oranges thrive in locations that are considered to have subtropical or tropical climates, your trees must be planted in a location that receives full sun throughout the day.

- **Harvest time**: The longer the fruit stays on the tree, the more the acidity of the oranges in neutralized, especially in cooler weather. To ensure your oranges are at the peak of sweetness, let them stay on the tree through the early weeks of winter.

- **The variety of the orange**: A tree that produces sweet oranges will not produce the best fruit it can until it has been established for several years. Older orange trees will offer the sweetest tasting fruits.

- **Fertilization:** For the best tasting fruits, proper amounts of fertilizer are necessary. Too much fertilizer may result in smaller yields, while not enough nitrogen-based fertilizer will produce fruit that doesn't taste as sweet as it should. The proper balances applied during the entire growing season will provide the best tasting fruit. Remember to avoid fertilizing the tree until its roots are established and the tree is growing.

- **Weeding:** Weeds, grass and mulch should be cleared from the tree frequently. Pests and rodents will nest in mulch and unkempt weeds or grass and can damage your tree.

- **Pruning:** As a rule, pruning is only necessary to remove dead or diseased branches. Excessive pruning for shape can have a negative effect on the tree and turn its fruit sour.

- **Irrigation:** While regular, frequent watering is necessary for young trees, older trees should only be watered far less. Once every two or three weeks is plenty for your orange tree; if you water the tree too often, the fruit will lose its sweetness.

- **Soil:** If you planted your orange tree in a clay soil, the tree will not be able to develop a strong system. Orange trees prefer a loamy soil; if the soil is too heavy, the tree will not be able to produce healthy, sweet tasting fruits.

Special Considerations for Container Gardening

Gardeners who don't have a lot of space but still want to grow their own food or beautiful flowers and plants will often turn to container gardening, and some orange tree varieties will thrive in containers. Container gardening is also a great solution to bring the beauty and functionality of outdoor plants and trees inside the home. While this is a perfect answer for gardening in limited spaces, plants grown in containers have special needs because they are completely restricted inside their pots.

Growing Citrus Indoors

You can enjoy your own citrus fruits from a container inside your home with a little extra attention. In addition to producing fruit, the trees will also fill the air with the light, sweet scent of their blossoms. While most varieties of tangerines and oranges need to be kept in a heated growing climate, there are some citrus trees that can thrive indoors in a very sunny location near a window. Before choosing a variety of citrus tree to grow in a container, make sure to check exactly how large the tree will grow in its maturity. It's helpful to purchase a tree from a local greenhouse or nursery that is already two to three years old. Trees this age are usually already three feet high. Measure the root ball and find a container that is only a few inches bigger than the root system. Citrus trees that will thrive indoors in containers include:

- Improved Meyer Lemon
- Persian Lime
- Calamondin Orange
- Rangpur Lime
- Eureka Lemon
- Meiwa Kumquat
- Otaheite Orange
- Kaffir Lime
- Eustis Limequat
- Nippon Orangequat

Planting Your Tree

1. Check your container for drainage holes. If necessary, you can add your own holes with a drill or a hammer and large nail, depending on the pot's construction material. Most containers will already have sufficient drainage holes in the bottom.

2. Place a water collection saucer under the container: Most containers also come with a saucer or water collection dish under them. If your container doesn't, find a saucer that is a bit larger in diameter than the container you will be using. Before planting your tree, place some pebbles or stones to the saucer and add water to them. The tree will benefit from the water as it evaporates, but it will not have a drenched root system.

3. Line the bottom of the pot: Cut a piece of the landscaper's cloth, or weed-block, to fit over the bottom. This allows excess water to drain while keeping the soil from washing out through the drainage holes.

4. Add soil: Fill the container to the halfway point with either commercially made potting soil or mix your own from soil and a nutrient rich compost or other organic materials.

5. Spread the root system: Gently pull the tree from its pot and spread the root system before planting the tree in its new container.

6. Cover the roots: Put the root ball into the planter and add soil until only the root system is completely covered. Leave the entire trunk above the soil line.

7. Water your newly planted tree: Water your young container tree thoroughly, without drowning the roots.

8. Mist your tree: In addition to regular watering, you should mist your indoor trees on a regular basis to keep the leaves moist. The drier your home, the more frequently you should mist the leaves.

9. Mulch is not needed: Unless you are using mulch as a decorating factor, it isn't necessary to use mulch for indoor plants. You can get creative and dress up your indoor containers in many ways, such as using decorative stone, clay, sand, shells and mulches.

10. Thin the fruit clusters: When your indoor tree is showing clusters of small fruit, remove 2/3 of the fruit to encourage the remaining ones to grow larger.

Proper Sunlight Exposure

Citrus trees enjoy between ten to twelve hours of full sunlight daily. If your home can't provide a window with that much exposure, you can purchase supplemental grow lights from any nursery supply store.

Your trees will need to be gradually acclimated to being moved from the outside to inside, or from inside to outside, unless you are only moving them temporarily to protect them from an extreme weather event, such as freezing temperatures.

Ideally, they should get 10-12 hours. Supplemental lighting in the form of high intensity discharge lighting can be used on occasion (depending on weather and your available sunlight which is determined by latitude).

Humidity and Moisture

Because citrus trees need tropical climates, they need to be kept in a humid environment, up to nearly 50% humidity. Without the proper humidity, a citrus tree will shed its leaves. Some indoor gardeners may find it useful to use a small humidifier to keep their citrus trees happy.

Watering your indoor citrus tree is necessary if the soil feels dry up to two inches in depth. Add water to moisten the soil, but don't allow it to pool around the tree; if the water saucer below the container collects water make sure to empty it to avoid drowning your citrus tree's roots.

In the winter, you will find that you don't need to water as frequently as you will in the summer; during hot months, you may find yourself having to water your citrus tree twice a day.

Correct pH Levels and Drainage

Your citrus tree needs soil that encourages enough drainage without drying the soil completely. Adding a few handfuls of loose gravel, about 1" to 2", before adding your potting soil is a great way to achieve the right balance for drainage. The potting soil should include one part of peat, one part of sand, and one-part vermiculite or perlite to encourage adequate drainage for your citrus tree.

For the most accurate monitoring of pH levels, go to your nursery and pick up a test kit. Your citrus tree requires a pH level of between 5 to 8.

Common Container Planting Mistakes

Container gardening is a little more complicated than throwing some plants into a pot and hoping for the best. Avoid these common mistakes and get the most out of your container plants.

1. Windy Locations

Container plantings and hanging pots are completely at the mercy of the elements, including winds that blow them around routinely. Place planters and hanging baskets in locations where they are protected from the worst of the wind, or they will lose their lush beauty and end up spindly, browning, or dying. If your containers or baskets look like they are getting blasted by unfriendly winds, move them somewhere else or even bring them indoors to give them a break.

2. Sky High Expectations

Your container plants have a life expectancy, so being overly sentimental and attached to a tree that is well past its prime is useless. The good news is that they can be replaced easily when they have passed their age of bearing fruit and become unsightly in their pots.

Citrus trees will not yield a harvest for quite some time after planting, so expecting a fruit bowl full of tantalizing oranges six months after planting the tree is unrealistic. Your commitment and dedication to your trees as they grow will pay off in the end, though.

3. Mixing without Matching

Don't go overboard when mixing your plantings in a container. A common mistake is to group favorite flowers according to the gardener's preference rather than the plant's needs.

Plants that have different requirements than their container mates will not thrive and may even die if exposed to temperatures and watering that are at odds with their own. Mixing plants is fine, though, provided the plants share the same needs for temperature, soil quality, and water.

When choosing plantings for a container, pay close attention to the light requirements. It is impossible to keep plants that have a need for bright sun alongside those that require partial shade; if you're uncertain, always look up light requirements of each variety before planting them together.

Most flowers have a tag with requirements, but if a fancy container that is already pre-planted catches your eye, it may already contain plants that have vastly different requirements.

4. Choosing Cheap Soil

Many times, gardeners believe that dirt is dirt. In container plantings, however, the quality of the soil you choose is very important. Because your plants cannot expand their root system and reach for more fertile soil, they are completely at your mercy when you pick their soil. Cheap soils may cause harm to your fragile plants, so make an investment in a well-draining soil that has excellent moisture retention and lots of nutrients. Choose a soil that is organic and combined with perlite, sphagnum moss, or vermiculite. Taking garden soil from your own garden is not recommended because it isn't sterile; it could be inadvertently contaminated with soil-borne diseases and weeds and not able to retain moisture as well as the commercially available bagged soil mixes.

5. Not Feeding or Watering Enough

Container plants will need to be watered every day unless the weather is cooler, or the rainfall is substantial. If your container has drainage holes in the bottom, they can't be overwatered. Your plants also need supplemental feeding with extra fertilizer or liquid plant food. Because your plants can't find nourishment and water, they rely on you to take care of them.

Plants should be fed with liquid fertilizer according to directions even if they are planted in a soil that contains a slow-release fertilizer. If you are away from home frequently, choose plants that don't need frequent watering or set up some type of an automatic irrigation system. Plants that need extra attention will stop blooming and their leaves will turn yellow.

6. Improper Pruning

Most flowers require some periodic grooming to keep them attractive and healthy. All fading flowers should be pinched to encourage the plant to keep producing blooms. Additionally, plants should be sheared to promote new center growth. Shearing with a pair of scissors or pruning shears is essential for plants that spread quickly or trail downwards, such as sweet alyssum or petunias.

7. Purchasing Showy Plants

Gardeners can get too excited over a lush pot full of blooms, but these aren't always the best choices when purchased from a nursery. As tempting as it is to buy one of these beauties, they are often older than you would think. Look for a plant that is still growing and not filled out completely yet; these are fresher and younger choices with a lot of life left in them, even if they aren't blooming when you first buy them.

8. Using an Improper Container

While there are numerous styles of containers for planting, it is important to choose the right one for your plant's needs. Clay pots, for instance, will tend to dry out far faster than a pot made of plastic or ceramic because of the breathability of the clay. Clay pots are best used for cactus and other succulents that prefer to be dry. Using a clay pot isn't entirely a wrong choice for other plants, but if chosen for them they will require more frequent watering.

The size of the planter is important as well, because smaller containers will dry out much faster due to the limitations in the amounts of soil that can be used in them. Choose the biggest pot that's still reasonably sized for your container plantings. Keep an eye on the average height of your mature plants; if they are over eighteen inches in height, they will need more soil and must be kept in a large diameter container to keep them from falling over.

Planting Your Citrus Trees: How To Dig for A Long-Term Happy Tree

Citrus trees are tropical and subtropical, and generally prefer to be in warmer climates. They will grow best in locations and climate zones with milder winters that stay well above freezing throughout the season, with very few extreme frosts. Citrus trees do need the cooler temperatures and shorter days of a winter season to keep them happy and productive. This is the time that the tree becomes dormant. The average temperature of a winter should stay in the 55-degree range for the best chance of a good fruit yield in the following harvest season. Navel oranges are especially at risk for small yields if the winter months are not cool enough.

Planting Tips

- Before planting your citrus tree, make a mixture of soil and 2 spadesful of kraal manure or compost. Add 250g of superphosphate.
- Make sure your new trees are transplanted to approximately the same depth that they planted in the nursery to avoid shock.
- Keep the bud union about a foot above the soil level.
- Tamp the soil firmly around the tree.
- Create an irrigation basin that is slightly larger than the tree itself.
- Water your new tree immediately on planting, and again the next day to ensure the soil is packed around the root system.

Encourage Strong Root Systems with Proper Irrigation

The roots are your citrus tree's nerve center, so encouraging them to grow strong is vital. In a healthy tree, the root system can grow to three feet in depth and six feet or more in width. Your tree's root growth can be restricted if there are soil layers that are heavy with clays and sand, or that are rocky and exceptionally gravel filled. If these layers are affecting the first three feet of the soil, the roots cannot grow down. The roots will then be bound by the confines of the heavy soil or rock layers, and unable to absorb enough key nutrients and water from the ground.

Whenever possible, dig past any rocky, constrictive soil to give the roots their best chance at spreading out.

Citrus trees do not thrive if they are planted in soil that is prone to being oversaturated. The signs of soil that provides a good balance of drainage and moisture retention is soil that has a clay content of no more than 10% to 40%, appears to be reddish, brownish or yellowish brown in color, and has no constrictive clay or mottled appearances below three feet in depth. These soils will absorb water and, in turn, pass the water on to the roots.

If a soil is prone to being waterlogged or oversaturated, it will block your citrus tree's roots from absorbing water efficiently. Soils that have restrictive layers or that will be problematic for the tree's root system will have:

- A Grey or yellowish-grey color
- A block, columnar, or prismatic structure
- Abundant yellow-brown or reddish-brown mottles
- Rock layers that appear stratified
- Both Soft and hardened mottles (concretions)
- A heavy clay texture

Watering your Citrus Trees

Newly planted trees should be watered at least twice per week until maturity, then a routine maintenance watering can be one time per week. As thee tree continues to grow, dig out its irrigation basin so that it continues to be larger than the tree's driplines. When digging, be very careful to avoid smaller feeder roots that are close to the surface of the soil.

The exact amount of watering the citrus tree requires will depend mostly on your climate, or the conditions during the growing season. If the soil is not well drained, the roots will become overly saturated which encourages root rot and will cause the tree to sicken and possibly die.

It is important to find the right balance of water for your citrus tree; too little water, especially in the late fall to early winter months will result in a harvest of fruit that tastes very acidic. If the lack of moisture occurs in the spring it will affect the blossoms and the fruitlets, resulting in a small yield. IF the tree was subjected to drought and then excessive rainfalls, the tree could blossom out of season and affect the setting of the fruit, resulting in smaller yields off season, and fruit that tastes "off."

A citrus tree can be suffering from water stress and not show any signs until its leaves begin to wilt and droop. By the time the leaves show signs, the tree is already distressed; don't wait for obvious signs of water stress. For mature trees, water up to 30 millimeters of water every week.

For larger scale citrus tree orchards, concrete canals and pipelines will provide irrigation. Most smaller scale operations will use a basin system and a dragline sprinkler system for irrigation of the orchard.

If a sprinkler system is used for irrigation, the trees will benefit from being aligned in a square shape; if not, the orchard is best lined up in a rectangular layout so that the most trees can be planted on each acre.

Laboratory Testing to Judge the Health of Your Citrus Trees

There are a few tests that can be routinely run in laboratories to make sure your citrus trees are growing healthy and strong. Only healthy trees will produce good fruits, so these tests are important in caring for your citrus trees.

Leaf sampling is the most accurate way to judge the health of your citrus trees. You can send leaves to the laboratory for testing annually using these guidelines:

- Valencia and midseason citrus: Mid-April

- Easy peelers: Towards the end of February

- Grapefruits and Navel orange trees: Mid-March

For the most accurate leaf sampling, only mature leaves, those around six months growth, should be picked. The leaves chosen need to have been on a fruiting stem, behind a fruit.

Gathered leaves should be placed into new, clean paper bags which are then sealed tightly. They should be delivered by hand to a laboratory within two days of collecting them; mailing these leaves will not provide accurate test results as too much time will have passed between gathering the leaves and the laboratory receiving them. If you can't deliver the leaves within two days, they can be stored in the refrigerator; never place the leaves in a freezer before taking them to the lab.

Leaves to be used for testing purposes should be:

- Gathered in the morning, but after the dew has evaporated from them.

- Taken from the same trees each year; you can mark your specific trees with some paint

- From mature trees that are fruit bearing

- Of the same cultivars for each test. If you have more than one cultivar, the tests must be performed separately for each one.

- Disease and pest free, living at the time of collection, and not sunburned.

- At least three or four leaves, each chosen from different sides of the tree.

- Representative of an orchard that is seven acres or smaller with the same soil throughout. Larger orchards will need leaves from different sections divided into approximately seven-acre segments for a total of 20 separate leaf sample packets.

For information on laboratories in your area that test leaves, call your local nursery supplier.

Soil Analysis

Citrus trees can be successfully grown in several different types of soils if they are well drained.

Typically, they enjoy a soil with a pH result of 6-6.5. The soil itself is the determining factor for the establishment of a healthy root system and how the tree absorbs the water. The soil should be tested before planting your citrus tree to judge its:

- Density
- Texture
- Depth

- Water retention, soil infiltration of water, and drainage of excess water
- Structure
- Erosion risks

An in-depth soil analysis will cover the chemical make-up of your soil, allowing you to make necessary adjustments before planting or to keep a mature tree healthy. To keep it simple and accurate, gather the soil while you are gathering leaves for leaf sampling. The soil should be representative of the entire orchard, or seven acres worth of land; if you know there are different soils in different areas of the orchard, they should all be tested separately and if your orchard is more than seven acres, the samples should be broken down into seven-acre areas and tested individually. The soil samples will be most accurate if they are taken in the tree basins, or the drip area, of the trees. For the most accurate results, move diagonally from corner to corner of your orchard.

Preparing the Samples for Shipment

- Approximately 2 kg of soil samples are taken from each section of the orchard and placed into clean, plastic containers or plastic bags.

- Never use a fertilizer bag or the test results will be skewed. Once each sample is separately packed, mix the soil in each sample completely for accurate results.

- Every sample needs to be marked with a label attached to the outside of the test container. Placing labels inside the containers with the soil can make them unreadable.

- Keep the soil samples from each section of your orchard separate. The subsamples taken from a certain orchard should be placed in a clean container (not a fertilizer bag) and thoroughly mixed.

- The label should include:

    - The depth of the soil sample
    - The number of the soil sample
    - The producer's name and phone number

For the locations of laboratories that conduct soil analysis, call your local nursery supplier.

Fertilization

As your citrus tree is growing and getting firmly established, nitrogen can be added to the soil every other month. One of these three will be most appropriate:

- 6 applications per tree annually of 46% 16 g urea
- 6 applications per tree annually of 36 g of ammonium sulphate (for measuring purposes, a matchbox of fertilizer is about this amount)
- 6 applications per tree annually of 28% limestone ammonium nitrate, 25 g.

After the first year, nitrogen can be applied twice a year, once in July and once in March. Potassium can be applied during the early spring weeks, and phosphorous can be added at any time.

Fertilizer must be spread under the canopy evenly and watered into the soil, paying special attention to the feeder roots that are growing near the surface so they can also benefit from the fertilizer before it is washed into the soil and out of their reach. In the Spring, as fresh new leaves are growing, the citrus tree needs micronutrients to address deficiencies of manganese, copper, boron and zinc. This is available commercially, or you can mix your own concentrate using three gallons of water and:

- 20g copper oxychloride
- 15 g zinc oxide
- 20 g manganese sulphate
- 10g solubor

Pruning Your Citrus Tree

As a rule, citrus trees do not usually require pruning for shape. Pruning your citrus tree will be focused on diseased or dead branches. You may also want to cut them back when they begin growing too large and are hindering other trees. Low hanging branches or those growing too low to the ground may need to be removed if they get in the way of collecting fallen fruit.

The ideal time for pruning your citrus tree is just before blooming or immediately following fruit set. Smaller prunings, like removing small branches and sprouts, can be done whenever they are needed, unless it is later in the growing season. Trimming too late in the season will encourage more growth which will be damaged by the frosts and weather extremes of winter.

After you have pruned, dab the area with a mixture of 50/50 water and white latex paint. It is recommended that you clean and sterilize any tools you used to prune your citrus tree to lower the risk of spreading a disease.

Tools of the Trade

For the healthiest pruning results, you should have these on hand:

Hand pruners:

To remove smaller sprouts that are too big to be removed by hand

Shears:

For those branches that are too big for the hand pruners but too small for a saw

Saw or loppers:

For clean cuts to larger branches.

Remove all sprouts by hand or with the hand pruners while they are still small enough to be snapped off. Never let the sprouts get big enough that the need to be removed with the saw or loppers. When removing sprouts, only remove it to the base of the sprout, leaving the branch collar (an area at the base of the branch that is swollen up from the trunk) so that the tree is still protected from disease and decay when they branch is removed. If you can't keep up with the growth of the sprouts, wrap the lower ten to twelve inches of the tree in white cardboard to discourage them from growing.

Branches that are 1.5 inches or larger in diameter will need to be sawed down. Keep in mind that your goal isn't to remove the entire branch; you still need to keep the collar intact. The most efficient way to protect your citrus tree when you are cutting larger branched is to use a three-part cut.

Part One:

Find a spot about six or twelve inches from the collar and saw about halfway through the branch, starting on the underside and cutting upwards to prevent the bark from tearing.

Part Two:

Make the next cut approximately three inches or so further away from the trunk than the first cut. Cut the entire branch so that it falls clear from the tree.

Part Three:

Cut what is left of the branch, the stub, all the way to the branch collar. Make sure the wood remaining has a healthy look. It should be a whitish yellow in color, similar to a manila folder. Dark wood indicates that the limb is diseased and the tree may require treatment.

Did that seem quick & painless? That's because it is! I find pruning to be rather relaxing, almost like a meditation.

Smooth cuts using this three-part method will not need to be sealed or painted.

Common Pests of Citrus Trees

Like all plants, citrus trees are prone to various diseases and ailments, as well as pests and bugs. Whenever possible, try to purchase trees that are hardier and resistant to disease. Citrus tree growers should always try to limit their use of pesticides whenever possible. When spraying to rid a tree of pests and diseases, natural pest eliminators will be affected as well. Wasps are amazing predators, but spraying pesticide will remove them as well. Without natural defenses, a cycle of having to spray the trees routinely is created. This is not only a costly venture, it can be hazardous to the grower. Most hobbyists will not have the proper protective equipment necessary to apply sprays such as respirators and specialized gloves, putting them at a very high risk for exposure to fumes and skin contact with these pesticides.

Common Pests

The following bugs are the most common infestation agents for your citrus tree. It is generally easier to prevent them than to eliminate them once an infestation has begun.

Citrus Psylla

Citrus Psylla transmits a potentially lethal disease among citrus trees called greening. During the citrus trees growth flushes that occur in the spring, in late summer and early fall, and again in late fall into early winter, the citrus tree is highly susceptible to Citrus Psylla infestations. Check your citrus trees during these growth flushes to make sure your tree is not suffering an infestation. If you determine that the tree is a victim of greening, you will need to eliminate the pest and treat the tree.

If your citrus tree is infested with Citrus Psylla, you will find visible orange to yellow colored eggs along the edges of the new leaves. After hatching, the nymphs will relocate to underneath the leaves where they will remain, causing a malformation of the leaves. These nymphs must be destroyed immediately when they hatch with a pesticide that has a long-lasting residual action because the eggs will continue to hatch intermittently.

Citrus Bud Mite

This tiny and highly destructive pest will hide in the buds and blooms of your citrus tree, resulting in deformed growth patterns and strangely shaped leaves, fruit and flowers. This pest will affect the growth of the tree and decrease the yield significantly.

Any citrus tree younger than ten years is highly susceptible to the citrus bud mite, as are mature lemon and navel orange trees. These trees should be sprayed annually to keep the pests away.

Red and Brown Scale

Both infestations can be eradicated by natural predators and parasitoids. Brown scale can be identified as a sticky coating, called honeydew, that will cover the affected tree's fruit and leaves.

False Codling Moth

This is the larvae of a moth that feeds on the inside of fruit and causes it to rot and decay. All fruit that is infested should be removed and destroyed completely, and any fruit left on the affected tree after the harvest should also be destroyed because infested fruit spreads more false codling moth larvae.

Orange Dog

These caterpillars primarily feed on fresh leaves from young trees. They can be identified as small, with a yellow and black coloring, or large, with a brown and green coloration. They give off a foul odor when they are touched. The best defense against the orange dog is to hand collect and destroy them. Orange dog is frequently a problem on young trees because it feeds mainly on the young leaves. The smaller caterpillars are black with yellow and those that are larger, green and brown. They can be destroyed.

Citrus Thrips

A citrus thrip infestation can result in distorted, abnormally thick leaves and young shoots. These shoots may blacken and fall off completely. Citrus thrips will blemish the rind of developing citrus fruits from the stem down, sometimes covering the entire fruit. The fruit will remain edible.

Fruit Flies

These pests are notoriously hard to get rid of and will result in decay of harvested fruits. The best way to eliminate fruit flies is by applying toxic bait directly to the leaves consistently from February through June, all the way through the growing season.

Ants

Brown house ants and pugnacious ants are devastating to your citrus tree's yields. There are commercially available chemicals to eliminate these pests. Apply these compounds around the trunk of the affected trees and on all visible or suspected ant nests.

Weed control is important for eliminating pests. Keep the area around the tree trunk and under the tree's canopy completely clear of weeds. Quikgrass and nutgrass are rapidly spreading, choking varieties of weeds that must be addressed quickly before they get out of hand. Remove weeds by hand to protect the shallow feeder roots around the tree, and if using tools such as spades, be careful not to nick the trunk or roots. A wound in the trunk or roots can lead to conditions that may cause root rot.

Common Diseases

Citrus trees are susceptible to several diseases. Some of these have devastating results for your orchard, so detecting them early is the key to successfully treating them.

Greening

Greening is caused by Citrus Psylla and is, as yet, incurable. It is more prevalent in climates that are cooler, and locations that are 600 meters or higher. Signs that your citrus tree is affected by this disease are yellowed leaves and bizarre looking fruits. The fruit from a diseased tree will be asymmetrical and misshapen, with one side growing normally and appearing to ripen while the other side remains small and green.

Because it tends to initially stay within one or two branches of the affected tree, early detection and removal of the diseased limbs is the most effective way to prevent the greening from spreading. If the entire tree has been affected, it is too late to save the tree and it should be removed altogether.

Citrus Black Spot and Scab

Citrus black spot is usually found in low lying locations with hot climates.

Scab is most commonly found on lemon seedlings. If your tree is affected by scab, young twigs and branches as well as leaves will look cork-like and feel very rough.

Both of these common diseases can be controlled and eliminated with chemical compounds.

A Parting Word

Growing citrus trees can be a rewarding experience. You don't need to have acres and acres of room; many varieties are easily grown in your backyard, in containers on your patio, and even in your house. Just remember that citrus trees are naturally grown in tropical and subtropical climates and will do better in full sun and warmer temperatures. Keep an eye on the delicate balance between watering and oversaturating the roots and the right nutrients in the soil.

With a little dedication and commitment, you will be enjoying your citrus fruits from your own backyard tree for years to come.

ABOUT THE AUTHOR

I was born in Eastern Europe where I was raised until the age of 10. During the summers, I would visit my grandmother's apple orchard on the outskirts of the city. It was a three-month period of the year that I would always look forward to. Nothing compares to spending time in the sun and enjoying nature with friends in the neighborhood.

This apple orchard is where I learned to ride a bike. It's where my grandmother practiced reading, writing and math with me. It's where I earned my cuts and bruises; climbing trees, swinging on the swing, digging around in the dirt and just generally being a curious kid.

As I grew older, my appreciation for the craft of tree maintenance has grown. I decided to learn everything that I could about this fine art. It turns out it's both fun and rewarding to have your own orchard. Citrus trees are unlike any other trees – they require special care.

My love for apple trees has grown – just like the trees themselves. That's when I started learning about citrus. Now, I want to bring that childhood joy to readers worldwide.

While there is much more to maintaining an orchard, this practical guide has just given you the foundation you need to successfully start your own garden. Even if you're operating in a tiny space.

Citrus trees can be grown successfully in greenhouses, too! Although they typically thrive under the bare sun, there could be soil conditions or weather patterns that may lend themselves to greenhouses. But that's a topic worth a whole another book.

I hope you enjoyed this practical guide to growing a healthy citrus harvest. Please remember to leave it a good review wherever you bought it (my guess is, it was Amazon) so others can discover this book for themselves when the time is right for them to do so.

Thank you.

Printed in Great Britain
by Amazon

43780700R00030